Lois Lorraine Covert
12155 SW Lynnridge St.
Portland, OR 97225

P9-DWI-240

THE CURE
FOR A
TROUBLED
HEART

THE CURE
FOR A
TROUBLED
HEART

Meditations on Psalm 37

RON MEHL

MULTNOMAH BOOKS

SISTERS, OREGON

THE CURE FOR A TROUBLED HEART

published by Multnomah Books
a part of the Questar publishing family

© 1996 by Ron Mehl

International Standard Book Number: 1-57673-017-4

Cover design by David Uttley

Illustration by Vicki Shuck

Printed in the United States of America

Unless otherwise noted, Scripture quotations are from:
The New King James Version (NKJV)
© 1984 by Thomas Nelson, Inc.

Also quoted:
The Holy Bible, New International Version (NIV)
© 1973, 1984 by International Bible Society,
used by permission of Zondervan Publishing House

New American Standard Bible (NASB)
© 1960, 1977 by the Lockman Foundation

The King James Version (KJV)

All Rights Reserved
No part of this publication may be reproduced, stored in a retrieval system,
or transmitted, in any form or by any means—electronic, mechanical,
photocopying, recording, or otherwise—without prior written permission.

For information:
QUESTAR PUBLISHERS, INC.
POST OFFICE BOX 1720
SISTERS, OREGON 97759

LIBRARY OF CONGRESS CATALOGING-IN-PUBLICATION DATA

Mehl. Ron.
The cure for a troubled heart : meditations on Psalm 37 / Ron Mehl.
p.   cm.
ISBN 1-57673-017-4 (alk. paper)
1. Bible. O.T.   Psalm XXXVII--Meditations.   2. Consolation--Biblical teaching--Meditations.   1. Title.
BS1450 37th   .M44 1996
242' .5--dc20   96-34703
CIP

96   97   98   99   00   01   02   03 — 10   9   8   7   6   5   4   3   2   1

To the precious people
I feel humbled to pastor.

For twenty-three years their love
and care have been a source of great
strength and joy to our family.

CONTENTS

ACKNOWLEDGMENTS

A simple thanks never seems appropriate when people have done so much. It feels as if I should do something special, like buy them a car, build a monument to them, or put them in pictures for all to see. The people listed below have been instrumental in settling my troubled heart so many times.

To the staff at Questar Publishers. Every time I visit their offices I sit and cry. Not because they're mean to me, but because I am always so touched by the staff's tender love for Christ. I never leave there the same.

To Larry Libby, who makes me wonder how I could have ever enjoyed life without his friendship. When I throw bundles of stuff his way, he's able to make sense out of it. He's a renowned editor and best-selling author, so he certainly doesn't need me, but I need him. I'm thankful he doesn't turn Ron Mehl projects down.

To Carol Bartley, one of the dearest and most gifted people I know. She skillfully read this manuscript, looking for errors, and in the end saved me a great deal of embarrassment. Every writer should have a Carol Bartley in his life.

I offer special thanks to two scholarly coworkers of mine, Greg Dueker and Keith Reetz, who did a series of word studies that shed light on this subject and had a great impact on the book.

10

To two women, Debbie Matheny and Gayle Potter, who keep my life in order and make our office such a happy and peaceful place to work.

And to the Mehl family: our sons, Ron and Mark, whose lives have so profoundly affected mine. And best of all, to my wife, Joyce, who has been married to me for thirty years as of June 17, 1996. I know I married way over my head, and I'm glad. I believe God either really loves me, or He doesn't like Joyce very much. I think it's the former.

PSALM 37

Do not fret because of evildoers,

Nor be envious of the workers of iniquity,

For they shall soon be cut down like the grass,

And wither as the green herb.

Trust in the LORD, and do good;

Dwell in the land, and feed on His faithfulness.

Delight yourself also in the LORD.

And He shall give you the desires of your heart.

Commit your way to the LORD,

Trust also in Him,

And He shall bring it to pass.

He shall bring forth your righteousness as the light,

And your justice as the noonday.

Rest in the LORD, and wait patiently for Him;

Do not fret because of him who prospers in his way,

Because of the man who brings wicked schemes to pass.

Cease from anger, and forsake wrath;

Do not fret—it only causes harm.

For evildoers shall be cut off;

But those who wait on the LORD,

They shall inherit the earth.

For yet a little while and the wicked shall be no more;

Indeed, you will look diligently for his place,

But it shall be no more.

But the meek shall inherit the earth,

And shall delight themselves in the abundance of peace.

The wicked plots against the just,

And gnashes at him with his teeth.

The Lord laughs at him,

For He sees that his day is coming.

The wicked have drawn the sword

And have bent their bow,

To cast down the poor and needy,

To slay those who are of upright conduct.

Their sword shall enter their own heart,

And their bows shall be broken.

A little that a righteous man has

Is better than the riches of many wicked.

For the arms of the wicked shall be broken,

But the LORD upholds the righteous.

The LORD knows the days of the upright,

And their inheritance shall be forever.

They shall not be ashamed in the evil time,

And in the days of famine they shall be satisfied.

But the wicked shall perish;

And the enemies of the LORD,

Like the splendor of the meadows, shall vanish.

Into smoke they shall vanish away.

The wicked borrows and does not repay,

But the righteous shows mercy and gives.

For those who are blessed by Him shall inherit the earth,

But those who are cursed by Him shall be cut off.

The steps of a good man are ordered by the LORD,

And He delights in his way.

Though he fall, he shall not be utterly cast down;

For the LORD upholds him with His hand.

I have been young, and now am old;

Yet I have not seen the righteous forsaken,

Nor his descendants begging bread.

He is ever merciful, and lends;

And his descendants are blessed.

Depart from evil, and do good;

And dwell forevermore.

For the LORD loves justice,

And does not forsake His saints;

They are preserved forever,

But the descendants of the wicked shall be cut off.

The righteous shall inherit the land,

And dwell in it forever.

The mouth of the righteous speaks wisdom,

And his tongue talks of justice.

The law of his God is in his heart;

None of his steps shall slide.

The wicked watches the righteous,

And seeks to slay him.

The LORD will not leave him in his hand,

Nor condemn him when he is judged.

Wait on the LORD,

And keep His way,

And He shall exalt you to inherit the land;

When the wicked are cut off, you shall see it.

I have seen the wicked in great power,

And spreading himself like a native green tree.

Yet he passed away, and behold, he was no more;

Indeed I sought him, but he could not be found.

Mark the blameless man, and observe the upright;

For the future of that man is peace.

But the transgressors shall be destroyed together;

The future of the wicked shall be cut off.

But the salvation of the righteous is from the LORD;

He is their strength in the time of trouble.

And the LORD shall help them and deliver them;

He shall deliver them from the wicked,

And save them,

Because they trust in Him.

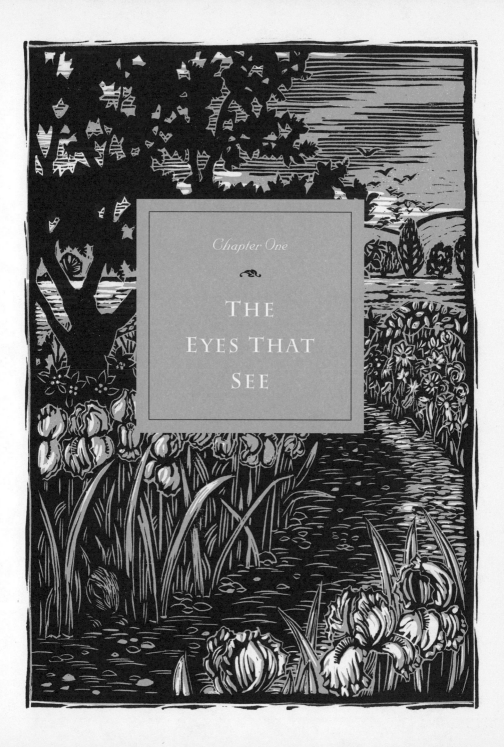

Chapter One

THE
EYES THAT
SEE

Then Jesus went about all the cities and villages,
teaching in their synagogues, preaching the gospel of the kingdom,
and healing every sickness and every disease among the people.
But when He saw the multitudes, He was moved with
compassion for them, because they were weary and scattered,
like sheep having no shepherd.

MATTHEW 9:35-36

THE EYES THAT SEE

he Son of David sat on a hillside with His disciples, watching crowds of people wind their way toward Him. His eyes scanned the multitude, and those sitting closest to Him must have heard Him sigh.

But did they know why He sighed so deeply?

The disciples, after all, only saw crowds. Jesus saw people.

The disciples saw a great throng, an unpredictable mob, a massive logistics problem. Jesus saw individual men, women, boys, and girls.

The disciples saw people as they were at the moment, trudging up a hillside in the morning sunlight. Jesus saw life histories.

The disciples were probably amazed by the sheer numbers of people seeking out their Master. Jesus was moved with compassion by the needs of each soul.

What sort of people did He see? He saw the blind, the disabled, and the poor. He saw the wealthy, the prominent, and the influential. He saw leaders and followers, husbands and wives, fathers and sons, mothers and daughters. He saw people who had edged very near the kingdom of God—right up to the threshold—and others who came out of curiosity rather than conviction.

But more than any of these things, Jesus saw troubled hearts.

Now if you and I had been seated with Jesus that day, looking out across the crowds, we might have seen evidence of unhappiness or worry here and there. A woman's slumping shoulders. A young child's cry. An old man's heavy shuffle. A frown. A shake of the head. But the Son of David saw more than that. He saw into the depths of minds and hearts. He saw abandoned dreams and withered hopes and hurts so profound they could hardly be contained.

Scripture says He saw men and women who were weary, torn, and harassed by life. He saw people who were directionless and help-less, like sheep chased by predators, with no shepherd to protect or guide them.

Outwardly, many of them may have appeared successful and satisfied. But "the LORD does not see as man sees; for man looks at the outward appearance, but the LORD looks at the heart" (1 Samuel 16:7). He saw *into* their hearts. He felt the emptiness. Felt the dis-tress. Felt the worry and anxiety. Felt the awful ache of loneliness.

Felt the weariness and discouragement that dragged on their spirits like an anchor.

That's the way Jesus saw all through the pages of the gospels.

…He saw the rich young ruler and loved him. And He saw exactly what was holding back that earnest young man from stepping into eternal life.

19

…He saw the woman at the well. Not as a Samaritan, or a foreigner, or an adulteress. He saw her thirst that went much deeper than a craving for water or fleeting relationships with drifting men.

…He saw His dear friend Martha, who always seemed so put together and in control but was inwardly "worried and troubled about many things."

…He saw Zacchaeus, a despised tax gatherer. But as Jesus came face to face with the little man who was scorned as a cheat and a Roman collaborator, He saw a deep weariness with life, an overwhelming desire to escape the pit he'd dug for himself, and a flickering hunger for God—ready to burst into flame.

Jesus is just the same today. He still sees. When John saw the resurrected Christ in all His glory—the way He appears in heaven right now—it was natural for the apostle to seek out the eyes of his old Friend and Teacher. But how startling those eyes must have been! John wrote, "His eyes were like a flame of fire" (Revelation 1:14).

These are eyes you can neither fool nor deceive. No one pulls the wool over these eyes…eyes that burn through all of our masks and masquerades…eyes that see motives beneath actions…eyes that discern sorrow beneath empty laughter…eyes that pierce to the depths of our soul.

Not long ago I got a call from Paul, a close friend of mine who pastors in another state. I knew immediately something was wrong. His normally buoyant voice sounded broken and strained.

His daughter, Kelly, a freshman at a big university, had just come home for spring break. It had been such fun to have her back—to have the whole family together again.

One afternoon while Kelly was out with some friends, Paul felt moved to do something "fatherly" for his girl. He would clean up her car, get it washed and waxed, and then take it for an oil change and lube.

As he was vacuuming the seats, he saw something wedged

between the seat and the console. An ID card. He didn't recognize the name on the card, but the picture looked familiar. Then it hit him. This was one of Kelly's older friends, who happened to look a lot like his daughter. Why would Kelly have such an ID card in her possession unless…?

A ripple of ice water went through my friend's veins.

Alongside the ID card, he picked up a ticket stub to a movie, the kind of movie he never imagined his daughter watching—or even wanting to watch.

Right after that, he found the roll of undeveloped film.

And that presented him with a dilemma. Kelly had always been an ideal daughter. Loving. Trustworthy. Obedient. She had grown up an active member of their church and its youth group and had never given her parents a day of trouble in her life. So naturally Paul wanted to think the best. The ID and ticket stub, after all, might be explained away. They might belong to one of her friends. *But what would the film reveal?* Should he find out? It would be an intrusion, and yet…

He thought, *Lord, forgive me if this is wrong. But if there's anything on this film that will help me understand what's going on in Kelly's life, I'm going to develop it.*

21

After Kelly had returned to college, he got the pictures back and looked through them. One in particular disturbed him deeply. It was a picture of Kelly lounging in a big beanbag chair with a bottle of beer in one hand and a cigarette in the other. She was surrounded by a group of guys—the kind that a father doesn't want his daughter surrounded by.

Heartbroken, Paul sat with the pictures in his lap and his face buried in his hands. So…all of that aura of "normality"—that simple joy of being home and resuming the old activities—had been a sham. Something manufactured. That really hurt. What bothered him most about the photograph wasn't the beer, or the cigarette. It wasn't anything he could physically see in the picture. It was Kelly's apparent attitude. It was the *ease* with which she sat there, doing what she was doing.

She looked very comfortable in that setting.

How could this happen? Why would she do this?

After he showed the pictures to his wife, Angie, and explained the situation, they decided that Paul needed to drive to Kelly's apartment at school and talk to her face to face.

He rang the bell and Kelly opened the door—so shocked she couldn't speak for a moment.

Finally she said, "What are *you* doing here?"

"I need to talk to you," he told her. "Can you come for a drive with me?"

They drove in silence, Kelly confused and apprehensive, her dad uncertain how to open the conversation. They ended up in the parking lot of a little church, under a streetlight. Paul wanted light in the car so he could see Kelly's face.

"I was cleaning your car while you were home," he began, "and I found some things." He handed her the picture. "Honey," he said, "is there anything in this picture that you think might break your father's heart?"

Kelly took the picture, looked at it in silence for a moment, and handed it back.

"Yes," she answered.

He wasn't really sure what he had been hoping for in that moment. Some tenderness maybe? Some remorse? A few tears? Yet when she looked at him, her eyes were dry. She seemed hard. Cold.

"You know, Kelly," he said to her, "when you step over the line and extend your borders, you'll keep pushing beyond the things you once believed and stood for."

He started the car and handed her the picture. "Here," he said.

23

"You take this. Go back to your apartment and put it up on your mirror. Every morning when you get up, look at it and ask yourself, 'Is this what God made me to be?'"

Paul wept as he parted from Kelly at the apartment. Everything wasn't fine; everything wasn't fixed. He embraced her, and she was limp as a doll. There was no embrace in return.

Both Paul and Angie grieved. For days Angie cried herself to sleep at night. These were the darkest times they had ever experienced as a family. All they could do was keep coming before the Lord in prayer, trusting in His care and faithfulness.

You and I never *really* know what's in a person's heart, do we? When the people in my friend's congregation greeted their pastor and his wife at the front door of the church, they didn't have any idea that their hearts were breaking. And Paul and Angie hadn't had a clue that their daughter was leading a very different sort of life at college than she had lived at home.

They didn't see until the film was developed.

But the Lord sees the undeveloped film. His eyes see into film canisters…and deeper still. His eyes see every corner of the heart.

For my friends, there was a happy ending. Several days later, Kelly showed up at home. She had seen how deeply she had wounded her parents, and the Lord had worked on her heart. She told them she had been wrong and how sorry she was for causing so much pain. She's still in college, but now she's studying with a purpose. She wants to prepare herself to serve the Lord.

Do you have a troubled heart today? Do you have hurts that others can't see? Wounds you can't even put into words? Aches that are years deep and reach into the back rooms of your soul?

Be assured of one thing, friend. Let me say again...BE VERY, VERY SURE OF THIS:

The Son of God sees.

And He is moved with compassion by what He sees.

The New Testament word for compassion has the term "bowels" within it. Both the Greeks and Hebrews felt that deep emotions originated in the bowels or intestines. That isn't so very strange, is it? After all, we might say, "I have a gut feeling about this" or "He felt it in his gut." And I don't think it would be inaccurate or irreverent to say that the Lord Jesus *felt it in His gut* when He saw a troubled heart.

And—whether you've realized it or not, whether you believe it or not—the mighty Son of God is moved by *your* troubled heart.

Don't ask me to explain it, because I can't. I can only tell you that the Bible says it is so. David had trouble comprehending this, too. Shaking his head in wonder, he wrote:

O LORD, You have searched me and known me.

You know my sitting down and my rising up;

You understand my thought afar off.

You comprehend my path and my lying down,

And are acquainted with all my ways.

For there is not a word on my tongue,

But behold, O LORD, You know it altogether.

You have hedged me behind and before,

And laid Your hand upon me.

Such knowledge is too wonderful for me;

It is high, I cannot attain it.

Psalm 139:1–6

We say with David, *How could this be? How could He see me and know me like that? How could He listen in on my thoughts? How could He know my troubled heart? I can't comprehend a God so vast and powerful!* You and I can't know what's going on inside those around us. Our eyes can't see beneath the reserved expressions and the carefully kept exteriors. We can't even begin to see what people have endured or are enduring.

I think of my dear friends Chuck and Lorna Bradley, members of our church in Beaverton and one of the most impressive, loving, physically striking couples I have ever met. Chuck is a former Miami Dolphin. He was the number-one draft choice coming out of the University of Oregon, and in his very first year in the league, his team won the Super Bowl. He stands six-foot-six, with the broad shoulders and muscular physique of a man who still looks ready to step onto the gridiron. Lorna graces the piano bench during our worship services, a truly beautiful woman as well as a gifted singer and musician. You could look at them and think to yourself, *No one should look that nice this side of heaven. No one should have such sweet spirits.*

To watch them walk into church on a Sunday morning, you'd think they couldn't have a trouble in the world. You would never guess the agony they've been through. But the Lord sees beyond the physical beauty and the outward signs of success. The Lord sees straight into their troubled hearts.

When their two-year-old son, Landon, was struck by a car and critically injured, the first thing that went through Chuck Bradley's mind was, *Who missed his assignment? Who messed up? Who did it wrong?*

It was a knee-jerk reaction for a former NFL starting center. Because whenever a quarterback gets sacked or a running back gets stuffed, somebody on the offensive line is in trouble. Count on it.

28

The first thing the quarterback, the head coach, the offensive coach, the running back, and about nine million fans want to know is *"Who missed his assignment?"*

More often than not, a player's number comes up. The television cameras zoom in on the guilty party, and the mistake is played over and over again in slow motion. Number Fifty-Two missed a block. He didn't even slow down that nose tackle. He didn't fill the gap. That's why that fragile, multimillion dollar quarterback was leveled like he'd been hit by a freight train.

Chuck knew all about taking heat for a missed assignment. As the center for the world-champion Dolphins, he was well aware of the need to protect the legendary Bob Griese and give him time to find the equally legendary Paul Warfield downfield.

So why couldn't he protect his little boy? Why wasn't he there to stand in the gap when the car came around the corner?

When Landon died of his injuries a few days later, Chuck felt as though someone was screaming his number. Somehow, in some way, it must have happened because of a fault in his life. Somehow he must have been responsible!

In his five-year pro career, Chuck had been on the receiving end of some unbelievably powerful hits. He'd been blindsided, he'd been steamrolled, he'd been scissored, he'd been injured, he'd been knocked unconscious. Most of the time, he'd been able to pick himself up, dust himself off, and go back to the huddle or hobble over to the sideline.

But no hit in all his life had ever hurt like this one. He couldn't stop blaming himself. And the hurt didn't fade with the passing of days. It grew harder and harder to bear.

Lorna hurt just as much. She had been there when it happened. She saw it all. The scene was imprinted in her mind in all its horror. Whenever she closed her eyes, she could see it. For weeks afterward, she was afraid to go to bed at night because she couldn't bear to see the tragedy replayed, over and over again.

The days were long and dark, and the nights were even worse. What do you do with that kind of grief? Where do you go? Where do you turn? Well-meaning people told them to lean on old friends, read books, take long trips, or sit in on therapy groups. But you can't run from that kind of pain. You can't bury it with words. And how could anyone really identify with their loss? How could anyone really understand their pain? So deep! So constant!

In the end they learned that only One could reach deep enough into their troubled hearts to touch them and bring healing. People were kind and sympathetic, but only Jesus could see, feel, and understand.

What does it mean to you and me that Jesus Christ can see into our hearts?

• It means there is One who is with us in our pain. *We cannot say we are alone.*

• It means there is One who truly sees and comprehends what we are going through and knows the true source of our distress. *We cannot say no one understands.*

• It means that there is One who feels the intensity of our hurts and is moved with compassion toward us. *We cannot say no one cares.*

In the pages that follow, David will walk us through a time in his life when he was confused and troubled. Typically, he spills it all out on the page. He works through his emotions and perplexities and comes through on the other side with unshakable conclusions.

There is a cure for the troubled heart. And it starts by turning to the One who needs no appointments, descriptions, or explanations. He sees. He is moved. And He will heal.

Chapter Two

DO NOT
FRET

Do not fret because of evildoers,
Nor be envious of the workers of iniquity.

PSALM 37:1

"DO NOT FRET"

 avid had struggled with a troubled heart for years.

Now, as an old man, as an aging king, he offers

his counsel. "I have been young," he writes, "and now

am old…" (Psalm 37:25).

As I read this psalm, I picture myself walking through the palace

gardens with old King David at twilight. He clasps his hands behind

his back as we stroll together down the palm-lined pathways in the

cool fragrance of a Jerusalem evening.

The wind billows his robe and ruffles his hair and flowing silver

beard. He gazes at the horizon as he speaks, watching the first stars

wink in the sky, just as he watched them so many years before as a

shepherd boy. When he turns to look at me, his eyes are full of wis-

dom. These are eyes that have seen great pain, loneliness, disappoint-

ment, and grief…but they have also seen beyond the pressures and

shadows of daily life.

David is a man who has sustained his life on the promises of God.

Psalm 37 is what Bible students call a "wisdom psalm." And isn't that what we need, when our life seems confused...when circumstances seem out of control...when our mind feels weary and our heart is aching? Just a little quiet wisdom and comfort from someone we can trust.

Sometimes people offer counsel right off the top of their heads. Their words are thoughtless and have no depth. They are words you can't depend on, for they have neither substance nor root.

When I was first diagnosed with leukemia, people would say the strangest things to me. They would make offhand speculations about possible sins in my life, or remark about my lack of faith, or take me aside to share some bizarre cure they had heard from a great aunt in Delaware. Already struggling with worry, I wasn't helped or comforted at all by their "counsel." It would have been better had they just said they would pray for me—or said nothing at all.

But David's counsel isn't like that. His words are never trite or thoughtless. When he prescribes a cure for a troubled heart, he knows what he's talking about. His words are not only drawn out of a deep well of personal experience, they are inspired by the living God. David had walked with the Lord as a simple shepherd boy and learned about his God through long, silent afternoons out in the meadows. He had learned from the Lord through the hard, lean years as a young man on the run, a lonely fugitive with a price on his head.

As we walk, David has things to tell me about what he has learned. He has counsel for me to follow. But before he tells me what I ought to do, he stops in the path and lays a weathered hand on my shoulder. Before anything else, he tells me what *not* to do.

"Son," he says gently, "don't fret yourself."

When we hear the word "fret," we usually think of worry in general. But David has something more specific in mind here. In Psalm 37, David recognizes that comparison and envy are major contributors to a troubled heart. Taking our eyes off the Lord, off heaven, off His provision, off His promises, we become worried and upset. Anger builds, frustration boils, and we begin to question God's goodness toward us—or if He really loves us at all.

The psalm begins with counsel for people who find themselves on the short end of the stick more times than they would care to count—and are just about fed up with it. David is speaking to people who are trying to cling to God's Word and God's ways through life but keep getting cut off by people taking shortcuts—people who care nothing for God or anyone but themselves.

Through the words of his psalm, David is gently urging us toward a different perspective…a long view of life, rather than a short view. But it isn't easy…

❧

Not long ago I attended the funeral of a dear friend named Mike. Mike was only fifty-three when he passed away. He had been a long-term, faithful pastor for years in a small-town church that could never seem to climb over the 100 mark in attendance. He studied hard and poured himself into his sermons. He stayed available night and day as an alert shepherd, visiting the sick, encouraging the weak, and giving himself away. When someone faced a moving day, Mike showed up to pack boxes. When someone needed help digging an irrigation ditch, Mike was on site with his work gloves and shovel. Anything to help. Anything to encourage. Anything to shepherd. Anything to show the love of Jesus.

But for all his efforts, the church didn't grow. Little by little, for one reason and another, attendance dropped. When the depleted congregation could no longer support them, he and his wife began managing a small inn. So in addition to studying for sermons and visitation, he found himself cleaning rooms, doing maintenance, balancing the books, and answering the telephone.

It was a lot to handle. Too much. Mike died in bed one night of a massive heart attack.

39

I attended his memorial service in the tiny funeral chapel. It was a small gathering. Some folks from the church. A few people from the community where he had poured out his life. His wife and kids. Joyce and me. There were no people of renown or denominational leaders. And only a couple of sprays of flowers. People might say Mike hadn't made a very big splash on the ministry scene. He was never on radio or television. Never written up in a magazine. Never had a column in the newspaper. Never wrote a book.

He just loved his family and gave himself for his little flock. In some people's eyes, that didn't merit much attention. In some people's eyes, that spelled failure. But I stood there and realized how much richer my life was because of Mike. His priorities were right: God, family, and ministry.

I went back to my motel room that night and wept. It didn't seem fair or right. He was a better man and a better preacher than I'll ever be. And from the world's point of view, he ended up with nothing.

If you think about it long enough, it's enough to make you angry. It's enough to make you a little bitter. It's enough to give you a troubled heart.

David says, "Don't let that happen, friend. Don't get caught playing the comparison game." And Mike didn't. Oh sure, he could have become frustrated or discouraged now and then just like any of us. That's part of the tuition for being human. But Mike had a life focus that locked into something beyond daily circumstances—no matter how pressing and distressing.

Mike was focused on the promises of God.

Mike understood that God rewards faithfulness...not fruitfulness. And God knows very well how to reward His servants in His time. I think Mike must have learned what David learned in the long, bitter years of running and hiding in the wilderness—that life can be lived on two levels.

On one level, present circumstances press in from all sides. As a young man, David's circumstances were anything but pretty. Oh yes,

40

he had the promise of kingship. He knew God's prophet had poured the oil of anointing on his head and that there was a promised throne out there…somewhere. In the meantime, however,…

> he was lonely,
>
> he was hungry and thirsty,
>
> he was in danger,
>
> he was afraid,
>
> he was weary,
>
> he was heavy-hearted,
>
> he was separated from friends and family.

From his hiding places, he could no doubt look out at the camps of the soldiers who were hounding him. He could smell meat roasting over bright, crackling fires. His enemies had warmth. They had food and drink. They had adequate clothing. They told stories and laughed around the campfire. They could go home to their wives and bounce their little ones on their knees. They were relaxed. They enjoyed job security.

David might have been tempted to think, *Just who is living like a king around here? Not me, that's for sure! This is a terrible life! It isn't right. It isn't fair.*

It must have been on one of those dark, lonely nights when he wrote these words:

My eye wastes away with grief,

Yes, my soul and my body!

For my life is spent with grief,

And my years with sighing;...

I am a reproach among all my enemies,

But especially among my neighbors,

And am repulsive to my acquaintances;

Those who see me outside flee from me.

I am forgotten like a dead man, out of mind;

I am like a broken vessel.

Psalm 31:9–12

~

That was one level. But there was another level of life, and again and again that's where David chose to live. It was the level of the promises of God. And through most of his psalms, you hear David moving from a focus on his present, painful circumstances toward a focus on the person, promises, and provision of God.

Listen…

> *For I hear the slander of many;*
>
> *Fear is on every side;*
>
> *While they take counsel together against me,*
>
> *They scheme to take away my life.*
>
> *But as for me, I trust in You, O LORD;*
>
> *I say, "You are My God."*
>
> *My times are in Your hand;…*
>
> *Oh, how great is Your goodness,*
>
> *Which You have laid up for those who fear You,*
>
> *Which You have prepared for those who trust in You.*
>
> Psalm 31:13–15, 19

43

When David had nothing, he still had everything…because he lived on the promises of God.

David and my mom had a lot in common. Whenever I was going through a difficult time as a boy or a young man, she would always tell me, "Ron, you need to make a decision. You must decide to live on the promises."

I knew what she meant. The promises of God.

"But Mom," I would say to her, "promises won't pay the bills!"

Yet somehow, through all those lean years, the bills did get paid. We may not have had much in our house, but we had God's Word, and Mom clung to it every day. In the back of her Bible, on the extra white pages, she did what a lot of the old-timers used to do. She wrote out God's promises. There were promises for healing, promises for provision, promises when you were afraid, promises when you needed direction. We even had one of those old "Promise Boxes" on the kitchen table, shaped like a little loaf of bread. It was stuffed with promises written on tattered and well-thumbed cards.

That sort of thing is a little out of fashion these days, and some might say the promises were quoted out of context. But do you know what? My mom lived on them, and they sustained her. And there was something else in the back of her Bible that meant more to me than anything. She had the names of all us kids written out, and after the name was a promise from the Bible appropriate to each one of us.

For as long as I can remember, my life has been linked with a promise of God.

To base your life on the promises of God, you must be convinced of several things. Hebrews 11 tells us that we must believe that HE IS, and that He is the REWARDER of those who seek Him (v. 6). God's Word shows us again and again that faith and obedience are the keys that unlock His power and blessing in our lives.

In what may have been his darkest moment to date, David faced the loss of everything at a little town called Ziklag, on the Philistine frontier. Raiders had swept through David's camp and taken everything. David and his little ragtag army had lost their wives, their children, and all their provisions. The men were so grieved and angry they talked about stoning him. What did David do?

David strengthened himself in the LORD his God. (1 Samuel 30:6)

How did he do that? Scripture says he "inquired of the Lord" (v. 8). He turned back to the Word of God. David had learned times beyond counting that when you lose everything you have, you seek God and His Word. You rebuild your life on His promises.

I was fascinated recently to hear about a unique form of Chinese puppet theater. Mr. Yong Fong, a fifth-generation puppetry expert, explained that traditional, Chinese, hand-puppet theater is acted out on two levels at the same time.

The lower level shows the characters as they progress moment by moment through the trials and tribulations of the play. On the upper level, however, the audience can see how the play concludes, as the villains are punished and the heroes are rewarded. Because the audience can already see the outcome by looking up, they're not overly worried when the situation looks grave and the bad guys start to gain the upper hand. Instead, they get vocally involved. They begin shouting encouragement at the harried characters on the lower level. "Don't quit!" they'll shout. "Don't stop! Don't give up! We *know* you're going to make it!"

That's the privilege God gives to His children. No matter what our present circumstances, no matter how gloomy the day or heavy our heart, God's Word tells us that His children will overcome. He will provide. He will comfort. He will heal. He will deliver. If not now, then later. If not in this life, then in the next.

Hebrews 12 tells us that even when we feel we're alone, we are surrounded by a great cloud of witnesses, who urge us to believe and press on. If you listen closely, you might hear David's voice, urging you to grasp the promises of God.

You *might* hear David. But then again, on that subject, I think he'll be drowned out by my mom.

Chapter Three

TRUST
IN THE
LORD

Trust in the LORD, and do good;

PSALM 37:3

"TRUST IN THE LORD"

ack in the seventies, a popular phrase made the rounds in Christian circles. You'd see it on buttons and bumper stickers and lapel pins.

"TRY JESUS."

For some reason, it always hit me as just a bit flat. Or trite. It sounded a little too much like "Try Dipsi-Cola" or "Try Chet's Frozen Dinners."

I will admit, however, that there are biblical grounds for a phrase like that. After all, in Psalm 34 David says, "Oh, taste and see that the LORD is good." God does seem to be encouraging people to "try Him out"…to wade into the waters of His goodness and grace and find out firsthand that He is everything He says He is.

But as soothing as wading in the shallows might be, real comfort and healing for a troubled heart don't occur until we get in over our heads and strike out for the deep. Real trust doesn't occur until we've committed *the full weight* of our hopes, dreams, and expectations—our very lives—into His hands.

"Trying Jesus" sounds too much like the fear of commitment so common in today's culture. Young men and women speak of "trying marriage." You know…if it works and it feels good, fine. But if it gets too hard or too painful or too dull or too confining, well, it's time to move on and "try" something else.

I remember our wedding day so well. Joyce and I graduated from college together on Friday night and were married on Saturday. This boy was so in love he didn't know if he was coming or going. What a fun courtship we'd had! We'd served on traveling ministry teams together and had gone to basketball games together (she was a cheerleader, and I was a basketball player). I didn't care much what we did as long as I could be with her.

But then something happened. I suddenly found myself standing at an altar before a pastor with a Bible in his hands, reading us our vows. He said things about "forsaking all others" and "in sickness and in health" and "'til death do you part."

That's when it struck me.

"Gosh," I thought. "He's talking about *forever*."

This was serious business. And I knew without a doubt that God Himself was watching and listening. This wasn't just hanging out with my girlfriend and drinking Cokes and playing Putt-Putt golf. The pastor was asking me to *make a commitment.* In fact, he was looking right at me and saying "as long as you both shall live." That's a long time! A lifetime. I was making a commitment to Joyce that would remain in effect as long as there was blood in our veins and breath in our bodies. This wasn't a trial run or a "let's see how this works." We were burning all our bridges behind us. We were joining our very lives together before God, and there was no going back.

Sometimes I have engaged couples tell me they'd like to write their own vows for their wedding. "Fine," I say, "but you need to have someone else marry you, because I won't." Maybe I'm getting bolder with age, but I draw a firm line on this. I've discovered that many of the "vows" being written today are syrupy, weak, and basically non-committal. Instead of saying "'til death do us part," they're saying things like *"as long as we both shall love."*

Now what does *that* mean? How long is that? Until the first fight? Until the first illness? Until the first dirty diaper? Until the first five-pound gain? Until the first wrinkle? Until the first gray hair? That's a line for someone who would be better off going to Hertz Rent-a-Ring instead of purchasing a wedding band.

The kind of trust David speaks about in Psalm 37 has commitment running straight through it—like the copper in an electric cord. One commentator describes it as a "submission to His will in the hope of His resolution of the dilemma. It speaks of an active obedience and reliance upon the Lord."

Try Jesus, yes. But to truly *trust* Him means putting yourself completely into His hands.

Psalm 37 is a beautiful picture of putting your trust in the Lord when all the circumstances of life are screaming something else. David looked around him, and at first glance it appeared that those who weren't trusting the Lord were doing much better than those who were. It seemed like whoever wanted to plan evil schemes and cook up dishonest scams were getting away with it—and prospering (v. 7)! The arrogant godless seemed to be growing in power, influence, confidence, and wealth, while the righteous in the land were just scraping along, barely making it (vv. 7, 12, 14, 16, 35).

But David had made up his mind. He was God's man, heart and soul. He was going to place his full weight on the Lord's faithfulness...come what may. That's trust. That's not only the kind of trust that brings salvation, it's also the kind that brings healing to a troubled heart.

❧

Whenever I think about trust, I'm reminded of the time I backed over the edge of a cliff.

Some of the macho, outdoorsy guys from our church thought it would be entertaining to have me go rappelling with them. It was one of those times when you're reluctant to refuse because you're afraid you might offend somebody.

I should have refused anyway.

I remember climbing for hours to get to the top of the cliff and then standing around for additional hours, waiting for them to prepare harnesses, check equipment, and tie off ropes. While they were getting ready, I ventured gingerly over to the edge of the rockface to take a peek. I could see the ground (through passing clouds), but since we were on an overhang, I couldn't see the face of the cliff at all. That's about the time I began to perspire.

Gentleman that I am, I let all the other guys go first. (Maybe a major storm would roll in, and we could all go home early!) But the inevitable moment came when there was nobody left on the cliff but me…and the guy holding the rope.

He motioned to me with a smile. It was my turn.

He cinched me in, and I gripped the rope like there was no tomorrow. You know, under most any circumstances, walking over the edge of a cliff isn't one of my favorite activities. But the most hideous thing about rappelling is that you have to walk over the edge of the cliff *backwards*. You can't see where you're going. And the moment comes when you have to step off terra firma into empty space.

That, my friends, is commitment.

I remember thinking, *Lord, if I fall, at least let me land on the guy who thought up this idea.*

As I looked one last time at the rope, at the special knot, and at the thick tree to which I was tied, I realized something significant. For the second time in my life, I was totally putting my life in the hands of another human being. Joyce was the first. And now there was this grinning bald guy in a flannel shirt on the other end of my rope.... I stepped off the edge.

That's the kind of trust David is talking about in this psalm. It's no weak "try Jesus" kind of dibble-dabbling in the faith. It means trusting the weight of your life to the rope of God's faithfulness, with no pos-

sibility of turning back. It's presenting your life to Christ as a living sac-
rifice—and refusing to crawl off the altar.

You aren't truly trusting until you're slightly out of control—like
Peter stepping out on the water. You aren't truly trusting until you've
leaned so hard on Him that if you fell, you could not catch yourself.
Trust means setting aside all secondary options, backup systems, and
emergency parachutes. Trust says, "I've gone so far now there's no
return for me. If God doesn't save me and hold me up, I'll go under."

57

Over twenty years ago, we began our ministry in Beaverton with a
small congregation. To be honest, I could have taken the whole church
and a couple of visitors out for pie in a Dodge van. On a good Sunday,
we had a dozen people rattling around in a building that would seat a
hundred and forty.

My problem right then, however, wasn't the smallness of the congregation. I felt terribly inadequate to pastor. I didn't feel capable of
shepherding even a dozen sheep.

I remember our first service, when I preached to those twelve people. It was a unique experience. One of the men who came through the door was dressed like an old trapper who'd just come down from the mountains after a long winter. Another man hummed. Not once or twice, but through the whole service. Really, it didn't matter much to me whether they *all* wore coonskin caps and hummed "Dixie." We needed every person there and were plenty glad to have them.

58

Still, I felt so insufficient for the task. The moment the service was over, I wanted to be alone. I walked into one of the side rooms, got down on my knees, and pressed my face against the cool metal of a folding chair. I was so troubled and burdened. I began to pray and cry out to the Lord.

"Lord," I said, "I'm in over my head and You know it. What can I possibly say to these people or give these people that will help them or change their lives? You know I'm not a very good preacher. You know I'm not Mr. Charisma or Mr. Personality. Lord, what am I going to do? What are *You* going to do?"

Joyce and I had been married for only a couple of years. We'd been youth directors, and then, amazingly, we were offered a good-sized church of four to five hundred people.

We were also offered Beaverton…with twelve people.

I thought to myself, *Boy, if we take the big church, we're going to look wonderful. If we just maintain that church for four or five years, people will say, "Boy, he's an awesome guy. He's got a big church."*

But what if God called us to Beaverton? (I had a strange feeling that He might.)

I sat down with my wife and said, "Joyce, let's talk. I want to know something here. I want to make sure you understand that if we take this church of five hundred, people are going to think we're awesome. If we just hold on to what we have and don't drive anybody away, people will say, 'Aren't they great?' But if we take a church of a dozen people and maintain a dozen people, they'll say, 'That Ron Mehl is a loser.'"

Joyce shook her head firmly. "Nobody would say that, Ron."

"Well, maybe not. But here's my real concern, Joycie. If we go to this little church, I don't want you looking around after a couple of years and thinking, *Why did I marry this loser? I could have married someone else—even a REAL preacher.* So let's make this decision together. If God calls us to Beaverton, it's possible we could end up ministering to twelve people the rest of our lives. If the Lord asks us to do that, are you willing? Because if you are, then I am."

I've learned since, of course, that you should never underestimate the faith and courage of Joyce Mehl. She was ready to take Beaverton in a heartbeat—or anywhere else in the world—if that's where the Lord was leading.

So…we took a deep breath and backed over the edge of the cliff. Together. We put our trust in the Lord to meet our needs and prosper the ministry as it pleased Him.

As the days went by, the Lord began to speak to me about our little flock. I thought I heard Him telling me that He was committed to doing a great work in Beaverton, but it was really hard for me to believe, because I certainly didn't believe in *me*.

Then one Saturday morning I had an encounter with the Lord that changed everything. I arrived at our little church building while the robins were still announcing the new day and the grass was wet with dew. I fumbled with the keys for a minute in the morning chill, then let myself in. The truth was, I'd been a bit discouraged that week about the church's prospects. I'd been thinking, *Lord, nothing's going to happen here. These are the greatest, dearest people in the world, but we're still only a handful.*

I went into my office but couldn't settle down. Restless, I walked back into the cool dimness of the sanctuary. The morning sunlight, red-gold and mellow, poured in through the windows.

And suddenly I found myself on my knees, weeping my eyes out.

It's difficult to explain…and I'm not sure I should even try. But in that moment I felt the immediate presence of God as never before in my life. Suddenly He was just *there*, and it almost took my breath away. I didn't just fall to my knees, I was *pushed* to my knees.

61

In that moment, the Lord spoke to me about doing a great work in Beaverton. No, it wasn't in an audible voice, but I knew very well what He was saying. And I also knew that He was committing to do a work in Beaverton *whether I was there or not*. He could do it with me, or without me. So He was offering me a choice. If I stayed and put the weight of my trust in Him, He would use me. If I left, He would use someone else. (And if He could use *me*, He could use anybody!)

It was an encounter I went back to again and again over the following months and years. No matter how I struggled in my ministry, no matter how many empty chairs I saw on a Sunday morning, I could go back to the time when I felt the overwhelming presence of God…when He spoke to me, and I wept before Him and put my trust in Him to work through me.

In Proverbs 3:5–6, David's wise son Solomon wrote:

Trust in the LORD with all your heart,

And lean not on your own understanding;

In all your ways acknowledge Him,

And He shall direct your paths.

There are conditional and unconditional verses in the Bible. This is conditional. It is dependent upon our obedience. In other words, He's *not* going to direct your paths, He's *not* going to make a way, He's *not* going to work things out...until you make a decision to trust Him with all your heart...until you lean your full weight upon Him.

Have you done that? Healing begins when you do.

In his gospel, John describes a crossroads moment in the ministry of Jesus. It was a time when many walked away from Him...and a few vowed to stay with Him no matter what.

From that time many of His disciples went back and walked with
Him no more. Then Jesus said to the twelve, "Do you also want to go
away?" But Simon Peter answered Him, "Lord, to whom shall we go?

You have the words of eternal life. And we have also come to believe and

know that You are the Christ, the Son of the living God."

John 6:66–69

I love that. Peter had already backed over the cliff. Peter had

already driven his climber's piton deep into the Rock, and his whole

weight was hanging on the strength of that Rock.

63

"Lord," he was saying, "You speak of going away, but where else

would I go? What else am I going to do? You've got everything I have.

I've given up my business, my old relationships, my old pleasures, my

bank account, my very life. I've staked everything on You…all my

hopes, all my dreams, everything I am and have. It's too late to look

for any other options, even if I wanted to."

That's trust.

Yes, Peter's words at that point were stronger than his resolve. He

would stumble badly along the way. He would fail and falter and fall.

But he would come back, too…more determined than ever.

Of course he would. Once you've found the cure for a troubled

heart, you hold onto it as though it were life itself.

And it is.

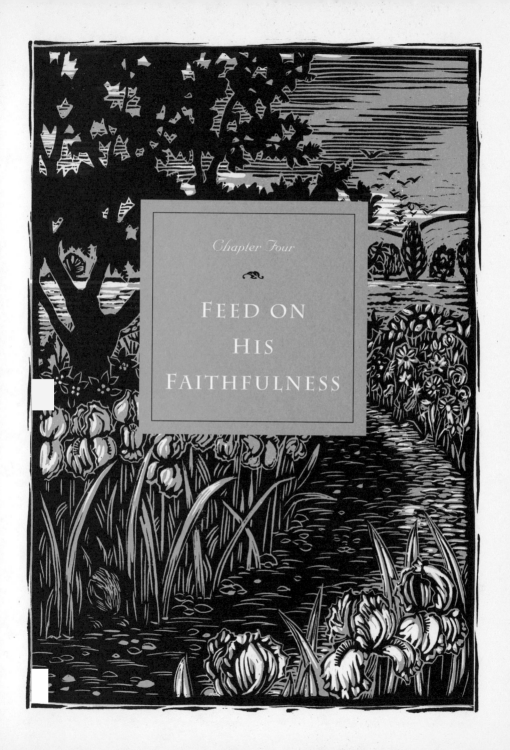

Chapter Four

FEED ON
HIS
FAITHFULNESS

Dwell in the land, and feed on His faithfulness.

PSALM 37:3

"FEED ON HIS FAITHFULNESS"

T he orphans cried themselves to sleep every night, and the volunteers at the orphanage were at their wits' end.

Many of the children had been rescued right off the streets. And now, instead of eating out of trash cans and sleeping on doorsteps, they could go to bed at night with full stomachs, lay their heads on soft pillows, and sleep between crisp, clean sheets. For the first time in their lives, they had adults who really cared for them, protected them, and comforted them.

But still they cried.

Finally, someone had a flash of insight. The children were fearful and fretful at bedtime, not because they were hungry, but because they were worried about tomorrow. Yes, they went to bed with full stomachs, but they had no confidence that there would be food in the morning! Nothing in their brief experience of life gave them any reason to expect consistency, stability, or security. True, they had tasted kindness and provision today...but tomorrow? It might all blow away.

Tomorrow might find them on their own again…hungry, unloved, and alone.

So they wept.

As a result of the staff's discovery, the orphanage came up with a new procedure. Every night when they tucked the children into bed, each child was given a large bread roll that he or she could hold or tuck under the pillow. It would be there in the night if they were hungry. And it would be there in the morning, a reassurance of the loving care and provision that was now theirs.

From that night on, there were no more sniffles and stifled sobs. The children went right to sleep.

Our friends Bob and Gayle Potter experienced something similar as foster parents. Some of the children they've cared for through the years have come to them from unspeakably abusive backgrounds. The stories of neglect and cruelty toward these little ones break your heart. Some are children of drug dealers who have known nothing in life but fear and hostility and deprivation.

Little Sasha came to the Potters' home from such a background. She was a pale, thin, undersized six-year-old. And her wide brown eyes were filled with fear. When the authorities found her, she was

cold, hungry, bruised, and unable to trust *anyone*—even people as loving and kind as Bob and Gayle.

One morning not long after Sasha had come to stay with them,
Gayle noticed some coconut shreds on the counter. Now you and I
might not have given those little crumbs a second thought, but with
the everything-in-its-place kitchen Gayle keeps, the bits of coconut
immediately signaled something unusual. Then she noticed a little
more coconut on the floor, below the counter. And a little more in the
middle of the kitchen floor.

69

Gayle realized that the coconut shreds formed a loose trail. *Like
Hansel and Gretel's bread crumbs*, she thought. *I wonder where they lead.*

The trail wound its way out of the kitchen, down the hall, and
into a bedroom. Sasha's bedroom. That was when Gayle discovered
that Sasha had hidden food *everywhere* in her room…under the bed,
under her mattress, in her dresser, in her closet. All because she was
afraid that, come morning, there wouldn't be any.

At dinner, Sasha would eat like a sumo wrestler. But still, night
after night, she would smuggle food into her room—food that wasn't
particularly fresh by the time Gayle tracked it down!

In verse 3 of Psalm 37, David seems to be telling us that children of

God never have to go to bed at night wondering whether or not He will be there when they wake up. They never have to wonder about His provision. "Dwell in the land," David wrote, "and feed on His faithfulness." Or, as the NIV renders it, "Dwell in the land and enjoy safe pasture."

By the time he wrote Psalm 37, David had seen a lot of life. He had already experienced careers as a fugitive, warrior, and a king. In his heart, however, he was still a shepherd.

David remembered what it was like to lead a flock through the wilderness. He remembered how vulnerable and dependent those sheep were. He remembered the pleasure and satisfaction he felt to lead his flock into a place of safety and abundance...in green pastures...beside still waters.

Later, another psalmist, named Asaph, wrote this about David:

He also chose David His servant,

And took him from the sheepfolds;

From following the ewes that had young He brought him,

To shepherd Jacob His people....

So he shepherded them according to the integrity of his heart,

And guided them by the skillfulness of his hands.

Psalm 78:70–72

David had graduated from God's school of leadership—Sheep-Pen State. He understood how to lead people because of his experience with a bunch of woolly animals! And even now this thoughtful shepherd-king tells us to place our trust in a greater Shepherd-King: "Trust in the LORD, and do good, dwell in the land, and feed on His faithfulness."

That word "feed" is the identical term used for feeding a domestic animal. Instead of allowing ourselves to be troubled, worried, or led astray by our circumstances, David is urging us to feed like a humble sheep on the faithfulness of God...to graze safely in God's good pasture.

How do you do that? How do you feed on God's faithfulness? What does that really mean?

When we speak of the "faithfulness" of God, we're talking about the firmness, security, and stability of His character—of all that He is. In other psalms, David describes God as his "Rock," his "Refuge," and his "Fortress." In the New Testament, James speaks of a God in whom "there is no variation or shadow of turning" (James 1:17). Which means that there are never any eclipses with God. There's never anything that stands between Him and me. There's never a time when the sun of His love and His healing is going to be blocked from me. No matter what I see going on around me, nothing will stop Him from delivering to me what He has purposed to give.

We can depend on such a God.

We can find in such a God the rest, comfort, and peace for which our heart longs.

Pasture in His stability, the old shepherd is telling us. Graze on His security and truth. The world around you may change. The fortunes of some will soar while others will suffer loss. There will be ups and downs, highs and lows, sunlight and storms, wide spaces and tight places. There will be temptations to become frantic, running here and there, trying this and that. But you, child of God, just be at peace and rest secure. Feed on God's provision and rest in His faithful love and protection.

Enjoy safe pasture.

If He has provided for your needs yesterday and today, He will provide for you tomorrow. If He saved you yesterday, He will keep you today…and tomorrow and tomorrow and tomorrow.

While the Israelites were wandering in the wilderness, God's manna was there for them to collect every morning. They were not allowed to take more than they needed or to hoard it or store it. If they tried, it became rancid and wormy. Inedible. So every single night they had to go to bed with no food in reserve. And every morning the miracle would be repeated. They received their "daily bread" for that day only. But it was always there.

God is faithful, no matter what the situation. When you go to bed at night—even if you have nothing in your hands or under your pillow—even if there are no visible signs of success and blessing in your life—you can trust Him to provide in the morning.

Have you ever watched sheep? It doesn't exactly set your pulse racing. After all, what do they do all day? Eat and rest. Rest and eat. Eat and eat and rest and rest. It's not as though they grab a quick breakfast and run off to do a thousand other things. They pretty much eat all morning. And *then* what do they do? Run errands? Go into town? Patrol the fence lines? Plant more grass seed? No. They graze some more.

Grazing takes time. They stay at it, trusting the shepherd to protect them from predators and lead them along to fresh pasture when they need to move…and not before.

That seems to be David's message to troubled hearts here. "Just stay near the Lord. Stay as close as you can to Him. Don't run here and there looking for cures. Don't keep consulting this person, that person, and the other person. Talk to the Lord every time you think of it. Read portions of His Word and then chew and chew and chew on them. Stay in His truth. Crowd your way into His presence. Drink from His stream. Stay, stay, stay. And rest in His faithful love and care."

This medicine for a troubled heart isn't like a pill you swallow for an instant cure. It's more like insulin for a diabetic. It's something that will keep you alive and well for the rest of your life, but you need to have it and partake of it *every day.*

In chapter one I talked about our friends Chuck and Lorna. When their little boy was killed, they could find no relief for their terrible pain, for the hurt and grief. Only by turning to the Lord did they find help. Did the pain go away? No. But they allowed that crushing hurt to drive them into the Lord's arms every day. Every day they took their pain to Him. Every day they fed on His truth and drank from His healing stream. Every day they let Him dry their tears.

Lorna was so frightened to go to bed at night, because of the terrible memories and images in her mind, that she not only read the Bible before she went to bed, *she tucked it under her pillow and slept on it.* Like the orphans who took the bread to bed with them and slept with it under their pillow, this grieving young mother pillowed her head on God's faithful Word. And when she woke up in the morning, there it was. Another day's comfort. Another day's strength. Another day's provision.

Yes, there are still moments when the pain comes surging back. When they see a little boy who looks like their Landon looked…when they think about how old he would be now if he had lived…when something for some reason reminds them, and the memories come, piercing so deep.

What do they do? They go back to the Lord. They stay in His pasture. They feed on His faithfulness. Yes, there are some hurts that God can cure in an instant. There are some things God can fix right now. But other hurts linger. The death of a child…a prodigal son or daughter…the loss of a mate…a broken marriage…an injury or disease…financial failure…or any one of life's deep disappointments.

These are hurts and troubles that require His touch every day.

I remember a period of time as a boy when I was growing extremely fast. I was eating poor Mom out of house and home and growing out of all my clothes at a pace that must have alarmed her. Of course every boy loves that, and it was fun to dream of becoming a pro basketball player.

But the rapid growth had its downsides, too, and it wasn't just wearing "high water" jeans to school. Sometimes in the middle of the night, my shins and legs would begin aching so badly I could hardly stand it. Now, of course, I understand that it was no big deal—just common growing pains. But back then I didn't know what was happening to me, and I was worried as well as hurting. It would get so bad that I would weep with the pain. Unable to sleep, I would go downstairs and lie on the couch.

Mom would come out of her room in her bathrobe and sit beside me on the couch in the dark. She would rub my legs and shins real hard, and after a while, it felt better. Even though the pain didn't completely go away, it was great to have her there. It meant a lot to know that she was with me in my pain and that she cared so much. And the next night, when the pains came back, she would do it again.

She was faithful. She was always there. Not only for the physical growing pains, but for all the other pains a bashful boy experiences as he becomes an adolescent and tries to make his way in a hostile world. Mom was with me through those times, and I depended on her.

I'm reminded that when Jesus invited us to "ask," "seek," and "knock" in the gospels, He literally said, "keep on asking," "keep on seeking," "keep on knocking." Don't do it just once and then try something else. When it comes to a relationship with the living God, we must ask, seek, and knock continually.

And what does the Good Shepherd promise to us if we do?

"For everyone who asks receives, and he who seeks finds, and to him who knocks it will be opened." (Luke 11:10)

This isn't some temporary cure or fix. It's a life direction. For the rest of your life if you keep asking, seeking, and knocking, you will continually receive, find, and have the doors opened. Or as David puts it, if you keep grazing in His pastures, "verily thou shalt be fed" (KJV).

It's a continual work of God to day by day bring peace and comfort to a troubled heart.

Do you know what this psalm is really doing? It is leading us to reorient our whole lives toward God. Throughout the forty verses of

Psalm 37, David is showing us how to trust in the Lord and rest in Him *in the face of external circumstances that scream the exact opposite at us.* As we will see, David is teaching us to delight in the Lord, even when we cannot delight in everything going on around us. He's teaching us to trust the Lord, and not to fret. And He's teaching us to feed on the Lord every day of our lives.

This *is* a cure, friends. The only cure. And it works.

I have only to remember a Sunday morning some years ago when Amy, sitting at the grand piano near the platform at our church, sang "Great Is Thy Faithfulness." I sat there wiping away the tears, thinking, *How can she sing that? It doesn't seem as though God has been faithful to her at all!* It had only been a few months since her husband of eleven years had deserted her and run away with his newfound relationship. What rejection! What shame and hurt!

Through it all, Amy has learned to feed in God's safe pasture. That's why she can lift her voice and sing...

Great is Thy faithfulness, O God my Father,
There is no shadow of turning with Thee.
Thou changest not, Thy compassions they fail not,
As Thou hast been, Thou forever wilt be.

Great is Thy faithfulness, great is Thy faithfulness,

Morning by morning new mercies I see!

All I have needed Thy hand hath provided,

Great is Thy faithfulness, Lord unto me![1]

Amy, like David, could sing *in spite* of her circumstances. She had tasted of His faithfulness. She was resting in green pastures, beside still waters, where no predator could harm her.

The Good Shepherd Himself has seen to that.

---

[1] Thomas O. Chisholm, "Great Is Thy Faithfulness," © 1923. Renewal 1951 by Hope Publishing Co., Carol Stream, IL 60188. All rights reserved. Used by permission.

Chapter Five

Delight
Yourself in
the Lord

Delight yourself also in the LORD,
And He shall give you the desires of your heart.

PSALM 37:4

"DELIGHT YOURSELF IN THE LORD"

t's easy to be delighted when everything happens to be going your way.

I can remember a few golden, exceedingly rare days on the golf course when I just seemed to have "The Touch." I couldn't do anything wrong. The wind was at my back, my muscles were loose, my timing was right, my eye was clear, my stroke was strong, my putts unerring, and I could seemingly drop that little white ball wherever I wanted it to go.

Talk about delightful!

It's especially fun when you're golfing with your buddies, and you get to pretend like shooting a 72 is the most normal and natural thing in the world.

As your friends shake their heads in bewilderment, you say, "Why *of course* my opening drive went 325 yards and landed in the green. *Naturally* I sank my twenty-foot putt. Did you really expect anything less?"

You feel so good about life that you become a big spender and offer to buy everyone Cokes at the clubhouse.

But then there are those "other" times. Times when you feel as if you couldn't get the pesky ball into the cup if you were on the Bonneville Salt Flats and the hole was as large as a bomb crater. You

can't do anything right. The wind is against you, your muscles are tight, your timing is dead wrong, your vision seems hazy, your stroke is feeble, and your putts have a depraved mind of their own.

Those are days when you certainly don't want to buy the Cokes at the clubhouse. You don't even want to see the clubhouse. You feel like stomping off the course and saying, "This is supposed to be fun? Why do I do this? I'm *never* coming back!" Delight is the furthest emotion from your mind.

King David had been looking at the circumstances around him, and "delight" wasn't exactly written across the sky for him either. Careless, wanton, power-hungry people were swinging across the land like a wrecking ball. Good, decent people were being trampled. Greedy, unprincipled men and women were clawing their way into positions of power and influence—and it all looked so ridiculously easy for them. David's heart was troubled. Worry dogged his waking hours like a toothache.

These are precisely the kinds of days about which David says, "Delight yourself in the Lord."

In the language of the Bible, "delight" is a soft word. A feminine word. A word that implies responding to and luxuriating in the attentions of another. It is the picture of a new bride who has deliberately chosen to seek her happiness and fulfillment in her husband. She yields to him and finds delight.

Here's another way to understand it: *To delight means to step away from your own strength and find strength in another.*

When I was a boy, my buddy Raymond and I could strut around and act as cocky and confident as any other little boys our age. We were twice as brave (and probably twice as mouthy) when we were together than when we were by ourselves. Sometimes that got us into trouble with the older, bigger boys. They saw through all our bluster and demanded that we walk our talk.

On occasion, a couple of them were more than ready to put us in our places. These were usually guys from another neighborhood.

Guys who didn't know about our secret weapon.

Dave.

Dave was Raymond's very strong, very athletic big brother. And Dave wasn't just any big brother. He had a strong protective streak in him and didn't take his brotherly duties casually. He took it personally when he caught anyone giving grief to his little brother (or his little brother's friend!).

Dave would heed our call and step into our situation, casting a long shadow. In those moments, Raymond and I were more than content to let our "tough guy" image go by the board. We were delighted to stand behind Dave and watch him wreak havoc on our enemies. We loved the fire in his eyes. We were thrilled beyond measure to see him stab the air with his forefinger and hear him say, "If you EVER mess with these kids again I'm going to FIND you and make sure that you are VERY, VERY sorry."

The only trouble with that arrangement was that Dave wasn't omnipresent. He couldn't always be where we were. He wasn't always within hailing distance in an emergency, and in those days we didn't have beepers or cell phones.

But King David knew that we can *always* delight in the Lord. We can always count on His concerned presence. He is always within range of our faintest cry for help. And He loves to have us step out of our own puny strength and into His mighty shadow. He loves to have us find our delight and fulfillment and security in Him.

King David was as tough and courageous as they come (remember Goliath?). But he had no problem at all stepping back from his own strength and taking refuge in the Lord. In an earlier psalm he wrote:

> *O LORD, the king rejoices in your strength.*
> *How great is his joy in the victories you give!*
> *You have granted him the desire of his heart.*
> Psalm 21:1–2, NIV

That's the very same thought he is expressing here in Psalm 37:4:

> *Delight yourself also in the LORD,*
> *And He shall give you the desires of your heart.*

Delight means *to not be strong for yourself.* In other words, let God do this. And as you do, He will give to you those very things for which your heart longs. Pour your energies into delighting in Him, and let Him work things out. At some point along the line, you get the idea that God said to David, "My son, you don't have to make everything right. You don't have to work everything out. You're trying so hard to be a little god on your own. Would you—just for a while—put all of that aside? Would you step back from your worrying and scheming and trying to manipulate events…and just delight in Me?"

That certainly sounds good. But it might not be as easy for some people as it is for others. Some people are real doers. They're action-oriented Martha-types, who like to jump into a situation, rattle around, and make things happen. It is neither easy nor comfortable for them to yield control to another. Even to God.

My best friend, Roy Hicks Jr., was a very godly man, but he was also a "doer." Right up until his recent, untimely death, he was bright, competent, energetic, and liked to roll up his sleeves and get things done. It seemed to me he could do just about anything he set his mind to. I always felt like he could wade into a black-water swamp and organize the alligators into a hospitality committee.

So when Roy, who loved me very much, heard I had been diagnosed with leukemia, he naturally wanted to *do* something about it.

He used to call me every morning of my life, and after he heard the news, he kept saying, "Ron, I'm just sick about this. I'm so burdened. What can I do? Is there anything I can do? Is there any way I can help?"

What a great friend! It really frustrated him that he couldn't throw his gifts and energies and love into some sort of plan to help me out.

One evening he wanted to get alone and do some praying. He got into his Jeep with his little dog, Jericho, and drove out an old logging road into the woods, west of his home in Eugene, Oregon. He parked the Jeep on a wide spot and opened the door to get out. As he did, two things happened in quick succession. First, Jericho jumped out and ran straight into the woods, barking his little head off. Then, as Roy got out of the Jeep, he dropped his glasses on the road and stepped on them.

Great, he thought. *Just great.*

He walked into the shadowed forest, praying, "Lord, what can I do? There have to be some things I can do for my friend."

He stayed out in the woods a couple of hours, praying for me— but feeling no reassurance at all. Then it began to grow dark. It was time to leave. Roy called for the dog.

"Jericho! Jericho!"

But Jericho didn't come. There was no snuffling in the bushes, no barks, nothing. The woods were silent in the gathering darkness.

Oh boy, he thought. *Now I am in trouble. Jeff and Kay are going to be beside themselves.* He knew how much his wife and young son loved the little rascal.

"JERICHO! JERICHO!"

He called and called, but there was no response. If anything, the silence seemed to deepen.

Well, this is it. This is too much. I might as well go home. My best friend has leukemia, I broke my glasses, and I lost the family dog. All in all, it's been quite an evening.

He climbed back into his Jeep and drove home, feeling as miserable as could be.

Early the next morning he woke up and thought, *I'm going back.* He drove back to the woods and began hollering again for Jericho. But there was no Jericho.

Finally Roy gave up. What else could he do? He'd done everything he knew to do, but he couldn't find the dog. His friend had a life-threatening disease, but there was nothing he could do about that either.

He cranked up the Jeep and yelled one last time out the open door. "Jericho! HEEERRRE JERRR-I-CHO!" Just as he began to slam the door, he heard a familiar yelp and a scurry of little legs. Jericho came bounding through the trees out into the clearing, ran to the Jeep, and jumped up into Roy's lap.

Roy told me later how the Lord spoke so clearly to his heart in that moment. "See...don't worry. I found your dog, I can heal your friend...and you can buy your own glasses."

From that moment on, Roy told me, he felt released from his terrible worry about my health. He had placed me in God's hands (where I had been all along).

It's just a simple story, but I think it makes an important point. There is a lot we *need* to do about our situations, a lot we *should* do, and a few things we may or may not do. But there are times in life when we need just to step back and say, "Lord, this is too serious, too hard, and too heavy, and there's nothing else I can do. I'm going to direct my energies and emotions into delighting in You and let You work on my behalf."

God really loves it when we do that.

There comes a point when you don't know which way to go in the woods, you don't know which way to run, and you don't know which way to look. There are times when changing a situation is simply beyond your capacity and power. You really can't do anything about your friend's leukemia. You can't find everything that's been lost, heal everything that's been wounded, and fix everything that's been broken. But you can step into the strength of the Lord God whose "arm…is not too short to save, nor his ear too dull to hear" (Isaiah 59:1, NIV).

92

God loves us so much that every once in a while, He arranges circumstances that are simply too big for us to handle and too heavy for us to carry. His desire is not that these things should crush us, but that we would learn to find our help and delight in Him.

God is a giving God. He wants to give us the desire of our hearts. But there are some things you'll never experience until you are ready to receive them by His hand. You can't work for these things. You can't obtain them by being sincere, doing good deeds, working your fingers to the bone, or trying very, very hard. God wants to *give* them to you. And that requires an attitude of humble dependence upon Him.

I've seen so many men and women who became impatient and insisted on taking matters into their own hands. God didn't seem to be leading them to a life partner, so they lowered their standards and determined to go anywhere and do anything to find someone. God

wasn't prospering their business, so they compromised their convic-
tions and cut ethical corners to make it happen. God wasn't blessing
their ministry, so they pulled a bunch of gimmicks and worldly tricks
out of the bag to generate "success."

Some of these determined people actually achieve their goals. Yet
what a price they pay! So often they ruin their lives in the process.
They gain what they thought they wanted so badly...but there is no
"delight." There is only emptiness and regret.

I remember when we were building our new worship center and
a little bird flew in the open window. Of course it was frantic and
immediately panicked, caught in this foreign place. Several of us tried
to help the poor thing. It flew into the walls. It flew into the glass doors.
It circled around and around, exhausting itself and beating itself silly.

I wanted so much to help that little bird! How easy it would have
been if it could have just trusted me! All I wanted to do was help it
reach its goal. I knew where the bird wanted to be, and I had the
power to get it there. All the bird needed to do was to sit still for a
moment. It could have perched on my finger, and I would have gently taken it outside and let it go. But it wouldn't let me. It seemed
determined to beat itself to pieces.

It's the same way with you and me. What a terrible price we pay when we refuse the help of God and refuse to find our delight in Him. How He longs to help us and teach us and comfort us…if we would only be still before Him and wait on Him!

Near the end of His earthly ministry, Jesus looked across the city

of Jerusalem and His heart was broken. He saw what was coming for the city. He knew the terrors and sorrows and desolation in store for her. But the people would not turn to Him! They refused to delight in the Lord. Jesus just shook His head and wept.

"O Jerusalem, Jerusalem, the one who kills the prophets and stones those who are sent to her! How often I wanted to gather your children together, as a hen gathers her chicks under her wings, but you were not willing! See! Your house is left to you desolate…."
Matthew 23:37–38

And our houses are desolate, too, when we refuse to delight in Him.

Are you troubled in your heart? Is it possible you're trying too hard to make things happen? Is it possible you haven't stepped back from your own strengths and your own solutions? Could He be speaking to you even now, calling you to find your fulfillment and pleasure in Him?

Through Psalm 37, the Lord says to David and to us, "Those who reject Me may seem to prosper for a time. But that time is short! You know their end. They're not going to be satisfied with their gains. Their arms are going to break under the pressure of what they carry. You'll see them come and you'll see them go. You'll see them rise and you'll see them fall. But you, My child, delight in Me. And if you do, I will give you the desires of your heart."

That's a promise that can survive a bad golf day, a bad hair day, or any distressful situation life might deal to you.

Actually, it's more than a promise. It's the cure for a troubled heart.

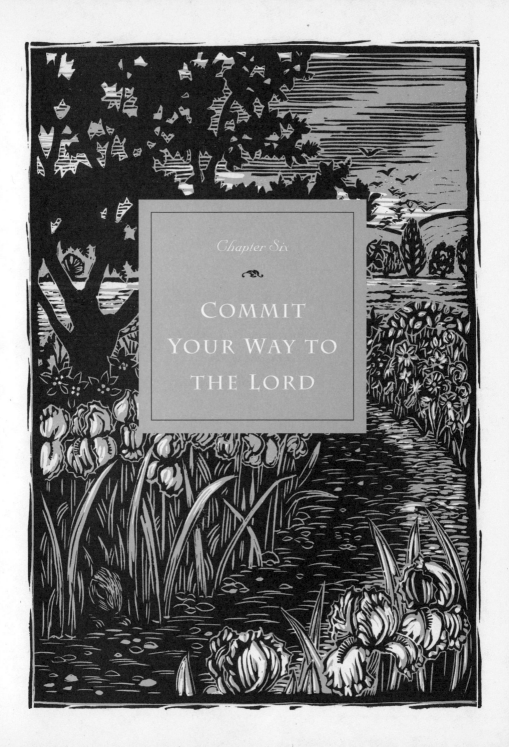

Chapter Six

COMMIT
YOUR WAY TO
THE LORD

Commit your way to the LORD,

Trust also in Him,

And He shall bring it to pass.

PSALM 37:5

"COMMIT YOUR WAY
TO THE LORD"

I t is a hard task to take your life in your own hands. It is a difficult burden to become, as the proud poet said, "the master of my fate" and "the captain of my soul."

It is a frustrating, heartbreaking job to be your own travel agent through the brief three-score-and-ten years of life granted us here on earth. Worrying and fretting over all of those details tend to take the joy out of the journey.

Almost every two years, Joyce and I lead a group of excited fellow travelers to Israel. It's one of the greatest privileges and thrills we have in the ministry. For many of the people who go with us, it's the trip of a lifetime. They've dreamed about it for years. They've scrimped and saved and sacrificed to be able to go. They've waited much of their lives for an opportunity to visit the Holy Land and "walk where Jesus walked."

You can't believe the excitement and the anticipation as our El Al flight from New York City touches down in Tel Aviv and our group sets foot on Israeli soil. The spiritual heritage of this land is so rich for believers that it's impossible to leave Israel without feeling you've left your own home. After all, it's His land, and that makes it ours, too.

A huge factor in the success of these trips is our link with an excellent, tried-and-true tour agency. Their experienced staff does a great deal of careful planning and arranging all year long, before anyone has even signed up for the journey. They work hard to obtain the best fares, the best connections, and the best arrival and departure times. They double-check to make sure we have good ground transportation waiting for our arrival, nice hotels to stay in, friendly, knowledgeable guides to lead us, and good food to eat along the way.

Beyond all those provisions and connections, Joyce and I have worked with them to plan a variety of moving experiences and awe-inspiring places to see. *Caesarea...Mt. Carmel...Megiddo, site of the future battle of Armageddon...a hike along the Jordan River...a sunrise over the Mount of Olives...a boat trip across the Sea of Galilee, where Jesus also walked...a solemn pilgrimage along "The Way of the Cross" ...a precious hour of prayer and joyous worship at the Garden Tomb.*

The tour company always does an excellent job for us, because they've done this many times before and seem to know what people

COMMIT YOUR WAY TO THE LORD

enjoy and appreciate most. They've been down those dusty Mid-eastern roads countless times. They've dealt with the airlines and the bus companies and the government officials. They know how to direct us to places that move us, intrigue us, and excite us.

On all our brochures, however, the tour company adds this significant line: *"Special note: The tour guides reserve the right to alter the sequence of the daily itinerary and make substitutions in order to meet changes brought about by weather, airline delays, or as deemed necessary for the best interest and overall comfort of the group."*

Do you know what? We trust them to do that. They have proven themselves trustworthy in a thousand different circumstances and situations. We count on them to take us here or take us there or tell us to jump on this bus or to wait for the next one. As far as it is possible, they have worked out the schedules and weighed the variables. And if something goes wrong, we rely on them to know what to do and where to go and who to talk to. For that reason, *we commit our way to them.* We roll the responsibilities (and the anxieties) over onto their shoulders and look to them to do what's best. We're "along for the ride," and everyone has the time of their lives.

Now imagine for a moment what it would be like if we stepped off the plane in Tel Aviv and said to those dear people on our tour, "Well, folks, we got you here, and now you're on your own. You have eleven days. There's a lot to see, so you'd better get after it. Meet back at the airport at such and such a time and we'll fly home. Shalom!"

Yes, a few of the more experienced travelers might possibly rise to the challenge, but most would be bewildered and deeply disappointed. They wouldn't know where to go. They wouldn't know what to do. They wouldn't know what tourist traps to avoid. They wouldn't know the best places to go or how to see what they want to see. They would get to the right places at the wrong times and the wrong places at the right times. Besides that, there are certain areas and certain buildings individuals simply cannot get into apart from an authorized tour. Following a tour guide allows you to see some things and experience some things not available to individual tourists. And even if these individuals did manage to see a few significant things, the experience would be so time-consuming and stressful that there wouldn't be much opportunity for quietness, or rest, or meditation, or worship, or companionship with new and old friends.

The bottom line, I guess, is that it wouldn't be much fun! Life is too short. A breath. A vapor. A fragile flower opening to the sunrise and wilting at night. I don't want to spend my brief life chasing down details and worrying over arrangements I was never meant to handle or carry. My way belongs to the Lord.

I can't help but think about the time in the Bible when Joshua was about to lead a tour group into the Holy Land. The difference was, he had about three and one-half million men, women, and children to think about, and not a single person in that vast multitude—including Joshua—had ever set foot in the land before!

What a comfort it must have been to have the ark of the covenant of the Lord moving out ahead of the whole party. The ark signified the Lord's presence, not only among them, but also out ahead of them. And since it was "the ark of the *covenant*," they were reminded that their Tour Guide was Someone who kept all His promises. Listen for a moment to the instructions the people received as they were about to cross the Jordan River and enter this strange, new land that would become their home.

"When you see the ark of the covenant of the LORD your God,

and the priests, the Levites, bearing it, then you shall set out from your

place and go after it.... that you may know the way by which you must

go, for you have not passed this way before." (Joshua 3:3–4)

Joshua was reminding them, "You've never been this way before, and neither have I! But the Lord goes before us. Let's be careful to follow Him and place our trust for this journey in His hands. We've never been this way before, but He has!"

It's the same with our lives. We've never walked this journey called "Life" before. When we open our eyelids in the morning, we face a day we've never lived before. When we celebrate a new year, we're standing at the threshold of 365 days that we know absolutely nothing about. We have no idea what a year, or a month, or a day holds. We don't even know what's going to happen in the next sixty seconds. The phone might ring with news that would scramble all of our plans and literally change the course of our whole life. We don't know what awaits us around every corner.

But *He* knows!

He's the Lord of time and eternity. He's the Alpha and the Omega, the Beginning and the End.

David wrote, "Commit your way to the Lord, trust also in Him" (Psalm 37:5). The literal Hebrew rendering is "roll your way upon the Lord."

It's the idea of getting rid of a heavy burden, of rolling it right off your shoulders. In other words, give Him the itinerary of your life. Don't try to do it yourself. Don't try to be your own travel agent and tour guide. Don't try to make all your own connections and reservations. Don't spend your life chasing misplaced baggage. Don't carry the weight and worry of all the "maybe's" and "what if's" of life.

That's a prescription for a troubled heart! Roll it onto the Lord! Commit it to Him. If you've trusted Him for salvation and heaven, your ultimate destination, why not trust Him for everything else in-between?

Paul had that very idea when he wrote:

He who did not spare His own Son, but delivered Him up for us all,

how shall He not with Him also freely give us all things?

(Romans 8:32)

In other words, if Jesus made our reservations and paid for our ticket to heaven with His own blood, doesn't it make sense that He will take care of us along our journey? We can trust Him! Jesus has been through life before us. He's walked the path ahead of us. Scripture says He "was in all points tempted as we are, yet without sin" and that He is "the author and finisher of our faith" (Hebrews 4:15;

12:2). He has faced the temptations, experienced the longings, felt the pain, and even walked into death ahead of us so that He might remove its sting. And after He did that, He went Home to prepare a place for us, getting it ready for our soon arrival (John 14:2–3). He's done it all. He knows how to be Lord over a life.

So what happens if we experience frustrating delays in life? What happens if we encounter blocked roads or rained-out events or sudden changes in our plans or circumstances? We can trust Him! We can trust Him to lead us safely through this adventure called "life"…and then all the way Home. When our flight touches down on the shining golden runway at Heaven's Interstellar Airport, and the light of eternal morning pours in through all the windows, we'll be able to say with the hymn writer, "Jesus led me all the way."

"Commit your way to the Lord" of course is the very opposite of our world's man-centered philosophy. Frank Sinatra's trademark song "I Did It My Way" sums it up well. And when "Old Blue Eyes" belted the number out before audiences of adoring fans, everyone would cheer.

And now the end is near

And so I face the final curtain,

My friend, I'll say it clear,

I'll state my case of which I'm certain.

I've lived a life that's full, I've traveled each and ev'ry highway

And more, much more than this. I did it my way.

It sounds good, I guess, when he sings it, but in my years of ministry, I've seen too many lives bruised, broken, and destroyed by that life philosophy.

I've heard husbands and fathers say, "I did it my way!"…as they left a brokenhearted wife and bitter, grieving children in their wake.

I've heard young women say, "I did it my way!"…and then spend the rest of their lives dealing with the consequences of an abortion or a child born out of wedlock.

I've heard teenagers say, "I did it my way!"…as they made choices that crippled their potential, stole their joy, and limited their future service to the Lord.

Frankly, I don't want to do it "my way."

I know how weak and fallible I am. I know how shortsighted I can be and how prone I am to take the wrong direction or the wrong path. Life is too brief and too precious to waste in a futile effort at planning my own itinerary and chasing my own baggage. I could have never made it to heaven going "my way;" it had to be His way, because He is the way, the truth, and the life. So if I'm trusting Him to get me to my final destination, why shouldn't I commit the *whole* journey to His care and keeping? It only makes sense.

In Psalm 37, David wasn't enjoying everything he was seeing on his "tour" through life. He was upset by actions of evildoers and those who threatened and bullied God's people. He was disturbed by powerful people who seemed to prosper and spread their shadow across the land. But in the end, He decided to fully trust the Lord. He decided to commit His way to the Lord and wait for Him to act.

Commit your way to the LORD,

Trust also in Him,

And He shall bring it to pass.

He shall bring forth your righteousness as the light.

And your justice as the noonday.

Psalm 37:5–6

So, David…you go to bed at night and commit your way to Him. What can you really anticipate? What can you really expect?

You can expect and be assured of this: If the Lord gives you another day of life, then as surely as the sun comes up in the morning, He's going to be working to bring about your righteousness and the judgment for which your heart longs. He's going to be working out all the details, and His eyes won't miss a single thing. He won't overlook your faithful trust in Him. And He won't overlook those who walk in pride and arrogance and seek to do you harm.

David has been fretting and anxious over the apparent triumph of the greedy and wicked. He's troubled by all the wrong he sees. But he hears the Lord telling him, "David, do you remember when you were a shepherd boy and watched the sun come up over the hills of Judah? Well David, as surely as the sun comes up in the east, I'll vindicate your righteousness and will bring things into balance and judgment. Turn loose of that weight you are carrying, and entrust it to Me."

In Psalm 55, it sounds as though David has learned that lesson well. He writes:

Cast your cares on the LORD

and he will sustain you;

he will never let the righteous fall.

Psalm 55:22, NIV

In all his trials and tribulations, the apostle Peter must have remembered those words of King David. Peter wrote to a flock of persecuted believers about "casting all your care upon Him, for He cares for you" (1 Peter 5:7).

The word Peter used for "care" literally means "to divide the mind." Have you ever felt that way? Have you ever felt as though your mind is going in a thousand directions, worrying about so many things you can't even keep track of them all? You're worried about the past, things you wish you could undo but you can't. You're worried about the present, everything that's going on in your life right now, making it seem like a three-ring circus. You're worried about the future; you see clouds stacking up on the dark horizon, and you wonder what storms might come sweeping down on you and your family. You wake up in the morning with so many things to do and to decide that you feel like crawling right back under your blankets.

Peter says, "Take all of that and cast it on to the Lord." Why? Because He really cares for you. He really cares about everything that happens in your life. He loves you!

David's son Solomon must have learned of this approach to life at his dad's knee. After Solomon assumed his father's throne and became king of Israel, he wrote these words:

> *Commit to the LORD whatever you do,*
>
> *and your plans will succeed.*
>
> Proverbs 16:3, NIV

111

And how true it was for Solomon. As long as he trusted wholly in the God of his father, his plans *did* succeed—and what great plans they were! He became wise beyond measure, wealthy beyond counting, and esteemed and honored all over the world. But when he turned away from the Lord and began trusting in his own wisdom and worshiping other gods, his plans didn't succeed at all. He led his whole nation into brokenness and disaster.

The truth is, God longs for us to commit our way to Him. He longs for us to trust Him with all of our heart.

I remember hearing a story about a little boy who was helping his father move books out of an attic office into more spacious quarters downstairs. It was important to the little guy that he was helping his dad, even though he was probably getting in the way and slowing things down more than he was actually assisting. But that boy had a wise and patient father who knew it was more important to work at a task with his young son than it was to move a pile of books efficiently.

Among this man's books, however, were some rather large study books, and it was a chore for the boy to get them down the stairs. As a matter of fact, on one particular load, the boy dropped his pile of books several times. Finally, he sat down on the stairs and wept in frustration. He wasn't doing any good at all. He wasn't strong enough to carry big books down a narrow stairway. It hurt him to think he couldn't do this for his daddy.

Without a word, the father picked up the dropped load of books, put them back into his boy's arms, and scooped up both the boy and the books into his arms and carried them down the stairs. And so they continued for load after load, both enjoying each other's company very much. The boy carrying books, the dad carrying the boy.

In the same way, God wants to carry you *and* your burdens. And He will, if you commit your way to Him. As sure as the sun comes up in the morning, He'll meet your every need.

Chapter Seven

REST IN
THE LORD

Rest in the LORD, and wait patiently for Him. . . .

PSALM 37:7

"REST IN THE LORD"

etwork anchor Dan Rather was a little out of his depth in a television interview with Mother Teresa.

Somehow, all of the standard approaches and formula questions felt inadequate for the task. And the little nun from Calcutta, sitting beside him so sweetly and tranquilly, didn't seem inclined to make his task easier.

"When you pray," asked Rather, "what do you say to God?"

"I don't say anything," she replied. "I listen."

Rather tried another tack. "Well, okay…when God speaks to you, then, what does *He* say?"

"He doesn't say anything. He listens."

Rather looked bewildered. For an instant, he didn't know what to say.

"And if you don't understand *that*," Mother Teresa added, "I can't explain it to you."

Did this good woman mean she never says words to God? I don't think so. I would imagine she has a rather active prayer life for her work of mercy in the streets and alleys of Calcutta. I think she was trying to make the point to a seasoned television celebrity that prayer is something more than repeating certain phrases or formulas. Prayer is more than an elaborate construction of pious-sounding words.

Prayer is the intimate communication between two hearts…yours and God's. Prayer is letting Him feel what's on your heart, and He, in turn, letting you feel what's on His.

You don't necessarily need words for that transaction. But you do need to understand what the Bible says about *rest*.

The word that David uses for "rest" in this psalm is rich with meaning. In a literal sense, it means to be "mute," like an individual incapable of speech. In a broader sense, it implies both "quiet submission" and "patient waiting."

When you rest before God, you must decide in your heart that He is in control—whether life circumstances are going your way or not. To rest, you must leave everything in His hands, waiting for Him to make things right.

When David came before the Lord at times, he came with an offended sense of justice at the way things were turning out in his world. He didn't like the headlines. He didn't like what he saw up and down his land. How could people be so hard and cruel? So heartless? How could they trample innocent people the way they did? How could they be so arrogant and conceited? Who did they think they were? It was maddening to think about! It really got to him.

It gets to all of us sometimes, doesn't it? The unkindness. The casual cruelty. The malicious gossip. The unfair advantage. The broken commitments. The lies. The betrayals of trust. The thoughtless snubs. The deliberate hurts. Sometimes we feel so angry. And then afterwards, when the anger burns away, we're left with the ashes of emptiness and depression.

In Psalm 37, David urges us to come before the Lord and set all those things aside. He invites us into an attitude of openhanded quietness before God.

Writing about this verse, Spurgeon said, "Hold thee still!" In other words, don't move, don't speak, don't try to explain or argue, don't murmur about your situation. Rest says, "I'm not going to complain about where I am and how I'm doing—or about how others might be doing in comparison to me. I'm going to be silent. I'll just rest here, believing in my heart that my Heavenly Father will do what's best."

◦❧◦

I'm normally very occupied and busy as I can be as pastor of a large fellowship—sometimes on the run seven days a week. Being a shepherd to these wonderful people is an incredible privilege and the very joy of my life. I love seeing this flock fed and cared for. It's a big task, much bigger than I am, but the Lord enables, and I'm passionate about it.

After my severe heart attack a couple of years ago, I had no idea what was going to happen to my ministry. During my recuperation, I found myself lying in bed in a quiet room, too weary to talk or even think. I knew the Lord was there. It wasn't that I was always thinking about Him…I just sensed His presence. I wanted to communicate with Him, but I didn't know what to say. Somehow, I couldn't form the words.

But even in that fog of weariness and weakness, I could sense the Lord telling me, "Be easy, son. You don't have to say anything."

He already knew what was going on in my spirit. He knew how I felt. He knew what I had been through and what I was going through. He knew the drifting, shapeless concerns I couldn't form into sentences. *What will I do? Am I ever going to pastor again? Will I get to go back to the church? How severe was the damage? Will the Lord take me home soon? What will Joyce and the boys do? Will they be all right?*

I knew it wasn't time to ask such questions. That would come later. For now, it was enough just to be quiet before Him, to be in His presence and wait on Him. I didn't need to explain anything to Him, and He didn't need to explain anything to me. I didn't need to know "why" or "how" or "when," and I didn't want or expect Him to tell me. We just spent time together, enjoying each other's nearness. I knew that my life was in His hands…whether I lived or died… whether I ever got up from that bed or not…whether I ever preached again or not. It was up to Him, and knowing how much He loves me, I could rest in that. In His time, I would know what I needed to know.

It will be that way with us, sometimes. There will be times when we are so troubled in heart or confused or grieved that we simply won't have any words. There will be times when we can't think of anything to say to Him, and He doesn't seem to be saying anything to us.

In times like those, God would have us simply quiet ourselves in His presence. And rest. Rest in His constant love. Rest in His faithfulness. Rest in His cleansing and forgiveness. Rest in the mighty refuge of Who He is. Rest in the fact that all will be well.

❧

I can remember times as my boys were growing up when one of them would be very troubled or worried or had endured a disappointment or hurt. Sometimes after he was in bed at night, I'd go and just lie down on the bed beside him. It's nice if you can think of wise, fatherly words in those moments, but the words aren't always there. It was enough just to lie beside my boy and be there with him.

In the old TV shows, like *Leave It to Beaver* and *Father Knows Best*, the dad (usually in a jacket and tie) would sit on his child's bed and say all kinds of profound, memorable things. But that's Hollywood. In real life, the words aren't always there when you want them. But you can still *be there*. You can still be close. You can still be a comfort and a companion by your very proximity. Your simple presence says, "I'm with you in this. I care about how you feel. I wish there was something I could do to help. I'm so sorry you're hurting. I love you very much."

Was that a trouble or bother for me to do, to lie beside my sons like that? Of course not! It was a high privilege. When you love some-one, you enjoy being with him or with her. You like being close. You cherish sharing that time, even if neither of you has a word to say. With all my heart, I wanted to be the kind of dad who took advantage of those priceless times.

And the Lord wants to be that kind of Father to you. A Father who is there. A Father who is active toward you, not passive. He *likes* you. He chooses to be near you. He has a trillion solar systems to run and galaxies beyond number to guide through the heavens. He has a lot of important places to be and people to meet and things to do…but He especially likes just to spend time—quiet time—with you.

In Psalm 46:10, the Lord says: "Be still, and know that I am God."

Another translation says: "Cease striving, and know that I am God" (NASB).

Have you taken time for that in your life in recent days? Have you come into His presence and, without saying a word, taken time to consider *Who He is?* How can you really do that when you come rush-ing into His presence with your heart full of worries and strife and your mouth full of complaints and fears?

"Be still!" He says. "Hush. Cease striving. Do you know Who I am? I am God. I am the Creator and Lord of the universe. I am the One who is all-powerful and all-knowing. I am the One who has always been and always will be. I am the One for whom nothing is impossible. I am above time; I live in eternity. And I am the One who sent My own Son from My side to buy you back from the kingdom of darkness and the slave market of sin."

Be still. Set your worries aside. Put your petitions down. File your complaints for a while. Tuck your long list of requests back into your pocket. *Think* for a minute about this One you wish to speak to.

In the little, frequently overlooked book of Zephaniah, the prophet speaks of a future day when Israel will enjoy the nearness of God with a full heart.

"The LORD your God in your midst,

The Mighty One, will save;

He will rejoice over you with gladness,

He will quiet you with His love,

He will rejoice over you with singing."

Zephaniah 3:17

Those are the kind of moments God wants to share with all of His children...if we would give Him the opportunity.

When I was dating Joyce in Bible college, I would strategize opportunities to be with her. I wanted to eat lunch when she ate lunch. I wanted to walk to class when she walked to class. Whatever her off-campus ministry was, I wanted to do the same thing. I changed majors to be in more classes with her. I changed churches to keep her close on Sundays. I didn't want her to have the opportunity to discover she could get along without me!

Jesus planned times to be with His disciples, too. They walked long distances together. They sailed across the Sea of Galilee on an evening wind. They ate together on sunny hillsides. They slept in ancient olive groves under still-more-ancient starlight. At one point, when the schedule was getting too harried and the pressure was growing too heavy, He said:

"Come with me by yourselves to a quiet place and get some rest."

(Mark 6:31, NIV)

125

Isn't that a beautiful invitation? Wouldn't you love to go back in time and take the Lord Jesus up on that offer? Can't you imagine sitting with Him under a tree on the banks of the Jordan? Can't you imagine just resting with Him there, knowing you are completely loved and completely secure in the presence of God's mighty Son?

Are you giving the Lord the opportunity to speak to you even here...and now? Are you allowing yourself to rest?

The truth is, you will never enjoy rest until you've finished your work. My mom, tired as she may have been, would never have climbed into bed if there were still dirty dishes in the sink. She wouldn't have been able to sleep, knowing that her work wasn't done.

What is our work? Our first work, as Jesus said, is to believe on the One whom God has sent (John 6:28–29). If we are to receive forgiveness of sins and eternal salvation, we must put our trust in the finished work of Jesus Christ on the cross.

But in the context of Psalm 37, what is our work? What is God asking us, through the psalmist, to do in these forty verses? David has the answer: "Don't fret...trust in the LORD...delight yourself in the LORD...commit your way to the LORD."

Then you will find rest—when you've finally turned to Him with all your heart and trusted every troubling fragment of your life into His hands. If you are still going to bed restless and troubled at night, if you are still turning the issues and worries of your life around and around in your thoughts as you lie in bed…you haven't finished your work. You won't be able to rest.

What a blessed sense of relief and release we feel when we truly understand and acknowledge that all of life is in His hands. From birth to death. From the turbulent teen years to the equally turbulent passage through midlife. From sunny childhood to the shadows of advanced old age. He is there. And if you allow Him, He will carry you all the way.

In Isaiah, the Lord says to Israel:

> *"Listen to me, O house of Jacob…*
> *you whom I have upheld since you were conceived,*
> *and have carried since your birth.*
> *Even to your old age and gray hairs*
> *I am he, I am he who will sustain you.*
> *I have made you and I will carry you;*
> *I will sustain you and I will rescue you."*

Isaiah 46:3–4, NIV

❧

I heard once about a dear, saintly old woman who was gradually losing her memory. Details began to blur. Once-familiar names began to elude her, and finally, even well-loved faces slipped from recognition.

Throughout her life, however, this woman had cherished and depended on the Word of God, committing to memory many verses from her worn King James Bible.

Her favorite verse had always been 2 Timothy 1:12:

For I know whom I have believed, and am persuaded that he is able to keep that which I have committed unto him against that day.

She was finally confined to bed in a nursing home, and her family knew she would never leave the bed alive. As they visited with her, she would still quote verses of Scripture on occasion. Especially 2 Timothy 1:12. But with the passing of time, even parts of this well-loved verse began to slip away.

"I know whom I have believed," she would say. "He is able to keep…what I have committed…to him."

Her voice grew weaker. And the verse became even shorter. "What I have committed…to him."

As she was dying, her voice became so faint family members had to bend over and listen to the few whispered words on her lips. And at the end, there was only one word of her life verse left.

"Him."

She whispered it again and again as she stood on the threshold of heaven. "Him…Him…Him."

It was all that was left. It was all that was needed. She couldn't recall the verse, but the word she remembered was by far the most important word in the Bible. She held onto the one word that is really the heart of the Word…"Him."

Real peace and rest is all about Him.

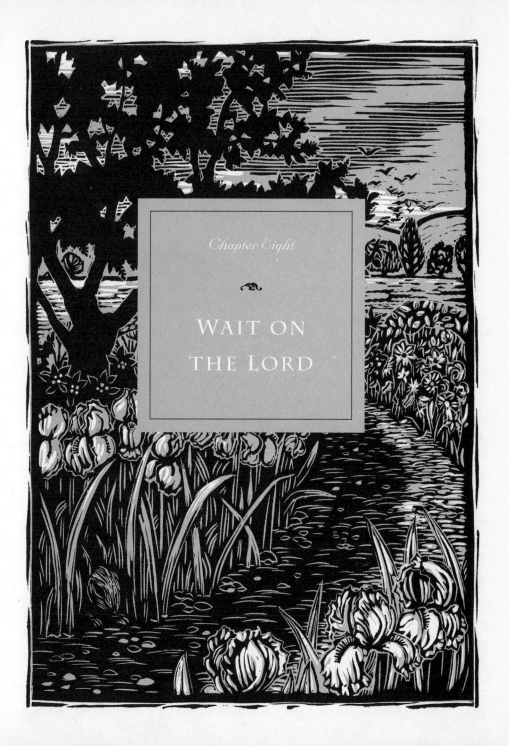

Chapter Eight

WAIT ON
THE LORD

Rest in the LORD,

and wait patiently for Him. . . .

Wait on the LORD,

And keep His way. . . .

PSALM 37:7, 34

"WAIT ON THE LORD"

Blair Martini couldn't remember her dad. Marc died unexpectedly when she was just a baby.

But she had seen his pictures. She'd seen the photos of him cradling her as a baby, looking down at her with adoring eyes. It seemed as though she could remember him…and she loved him with all the loyal intensity of a nine-year-old girl.

Last Valentine's Day, Blair made cards for the special people in her life. (And trust me, her cards are very pretty.) If her dad had been living, Blair would have taken paper, scissors, and crayons and made him a card to tell him how much she loved him.

But couldn't she *still* make a Valentine for him?

She asked her mom, Patty, who thought about it for a moment. Yes, she said quietly, Blair could do that if she wanted to. And Blair did want to, very much. So they went to the store together where the little girl picked out what she needed for the task.

Blair sat down at the kitchen table with all her things and made her card, taking her usual care to make it very special. When she was done, she solemnly asked her mom for a helium-filled balloon. This was a bit of a surprise, and Patty really didn't understand. But sensing this was important to Blair, she found one—a red one—and brought it home.

Blair carefully taped her card to the balloon and went out to the backyard. Patty followed, watching her little girl walk around and around, looking for an open patch of sky, free of tree branches and power lines. She didn't want anything to hinder the balloon's flight.

Hand in hand, Patty and Blair watched the red balloon sweep up into the blue winter sky. It became tinier and tinier, until it was a dot the size of a pinhead. And then it was gone.

Blair said, "Mom, I hope he gets the message."

She knew very well she would see her daddy again someday. Her mother had given her a verse from the Bible and told her that even though Daddy couldn't come to where they were, they could go to where he was (2 Samuel 12:23).

But they would have to wait. Perhaps a very long time.

Blair understood the waiting part. But in the meantime she wanted to send her dad a message that she would be coming along as soon as she could.

I think Blair understands the word "wait" in the way David uses it in

Psalm 37. When David employed the word in verses 7 and 34, he wasn't using it the way we sometimes do. When we talk about waiting, it's all mixed up with thoughts of boredom, or impatience, or wasting time.

Most Americans hate even the thought of waiting. We will change lines in a grocery store three times to find the "fastest" checker. (Only to discover he or she goes on break right as we step up to the register.) We will change lanes or pass to get around a "slow" driver. We'll walk around people on an escalator who have the nerve just to stand there. We feel tense or upset if someone doesn't show up on time.

Those are our thoughts about waiting. But not David's. When David used the word, he was thinking about *hope*. He was talking about looking for something with longing and eager expectation. In Psalm 37, David is eagerly waiting for God to deliver and reward the righteous, while dispensing judgment to the wicked. He is waiting for God to bring justice, and he expects it *soon*.

❧

A friend of mine relates a childhood memory about his little cousin waiting for his mom and dad to pick him up after visiting several days at his grandparents' house. The homesick boy sat in the old swivel rocker all morning, staring and staring out the picture window. From that window, he could see down the long, gravel road. He was watching for that telltale cloud of dust that would signal the approach of the family car.

After a couple hours of this, the grandfather came by and said in mock exasperation, "Doggone it, Bill, you're going to stare a hole right through our window!"

Bill knew who was coming that morning. And he expected to see that cloud of dust and the familiar blue-and-white '54 Ford station wagon roll up at any moment. He had no desire to play outside or even move from that chair. He focused all his energies and attention on that long, empty road.

Have you ever been in a situation like that...waiting and waiting with all your might?

Perhaps it was late at night on the curb at an airport terminal. Drained and exhausted from your travels, you fervently long for nothing more than to fall into bed. The hotel told you that the courtesy van was on the way...but so is Christmas! It's taking so long...you look and look and wait and wait. Every car or bus or van that comes around the corner has your earnest, eager attention.

Or maybe you've been at a crowded airport gate, looking and waiting for that one well-loved face among the sea of strangers getting off the plane.

The psalmist wrote:

> *I wait for the LORD, my soul waits,*
> *and in his word I put my hope.*
> *My soul waits for the Lord*
> *more than watchmen wait for the morning,*
> *more than watchmen wait for the morning.*

Psalm 130:5–6, NIV

Being a sentry on the wall of a city could be a tiresome, lonely job. (Ask any security guard or night watchman.) The weary sentries on top of the wall of Jerusalem walked back and forth, wondering when the long night would ever be over. At every turn, they would look off toward the eastern horizon, waiting for even the slightest indication of the approaching dawn. Did the darkness seem the tiniest bit less dense? Was there the slightest hint of gray, low on the horizon? Wasn't that dark clump of palm trees alongside the wall becoming just a little more distinct? Wasn't that a rooster crowing, somewhere in the distance?

How they longed for morning! And the psalmist said, "That's how it is for me, as I wait for the Lord. I've put all my hope in Him. I'm eagerly anticipating His touch on my life."

It's that expectation that keeps you, even when your heart is troubled. It's that knowledge that the waiting will soon be over and your desires will be fulfilled.

Waiting with eager expectation is an entirely different proposition from "just plain waiting." Do you know what makes all the difference in waiting?

It's knowing whom you are waiting for!

And when you think about Psalm 37, please don't think about sitting in the lobby of a dentist's office, waiting for your name to be called. Think about little Blair waiting through the tears and the years to see her daddy again. Think about a groom, standing at the altar, waiting for his bride to come down the aisle...waiting for that blessed new life together that is now so near!

Centuries after King David penned Psalm 37, the prophet Isaiah wrote about waiting, too. And I think he understood the word the way that Blair and David understood it. "Those who wait on the LORD," he wrote, "shall renew their strength" (Isaiah 40:31).

Do you know why that familiar verse comes near the end of Isaiah chapter 40? It's because he spends the first thirty verses describing exactly Who it is we're waiting for!

- He is a God who revealed Himself in Christ—and will reveal Himself yet again. (vv. 3–5)

- He is a God whose Word stands forever. (vv. 6–8)

- He is a God who will one day rule our poor, bruised planet with a strong, righteous hand and will reward His own beyond imagination. (v. 10)

- He is a God who guards and cares for His lambs like a tender-hearted shepherd. (v. 11)

- He is a God so big He has measured the heavens with His hand, has named every star in the countless galaxies of the universe, and directs their fiery courses through the pathways of space. (vv. 12, 26)

- He is a God who has all knowledge and complete wisdom. (vv. 13–14)

- He is a God who never overlooks our needs, never becomes weary, and never fails to note or understand our heart's desires. (vv. 27–28)

- He is a God who gives power to the weak and strength to the weary. (vv. 29–30)

In other words, this is a God with the cure for a troubled heart. And if anyone was *ever* worth waiting for, He is.

By the way, if you happen to find a red balloon with a very fancy but somewhat weathered card taped on to it, please forward it on. A little girl named Blair is waiting with eager expectation to see her Valentine again…and so she will.

But in the meantime, she wants to keep in touch.